T0198595

My Life as a Lesbian

Was love that hard to find?

Janice Estelle Pruse

MY LIFE AS A LESBIAN
WAS LOVE THAT HARD TO FIND?

iUniverse books may be ordered through booksellers or by contacting:

iUniverse
1663 Liberty Drive
Bloomington, IN 47403
www.iuniverse.com
844-349-9409

Because of the dynamic nature of the Internet, any web addresses or links contained in this book may have changed since publication and may no longer be valid. The views expressed in this work are solely those of the author and do not necessarily reflect the views of the publisher, and the publisher hereby disclaims any responsibility for them.

Any people depicted in stock imagery provided by Getty Images are models, and such images are being used for illustrative purposes only.
Certain stock imagery © Getty Images.

Scriptures Quotations are from the Good News Bible © 1994 published by the Bible Societies/HarperCollins Publishers Ltd UK, Good News Bible © American Bible Society 1966, 1971, 1976, 1992. Used with permission.

ISBN: 978-1-6632-4649-3 (sc)
ISBN: 978-1-6632-4650-9 (e)

Library of Congress Control Number: 2022918572

Print information available on the last page.

iUniverse rev. date: 11/04/2022

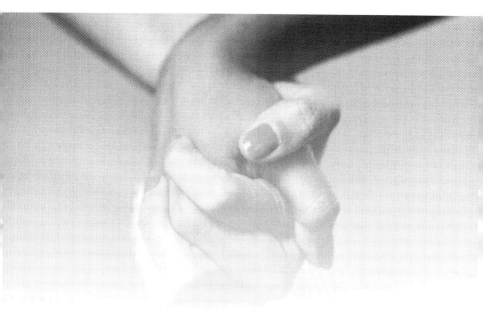

I am a lesbian, whose life was much of a shambled; my younger days before I got into relationships were easy. There was nothing to worry about, but what I was going to do the next day. Our parents took all the worries and problems so that we could have a good and happy childhood life; until the day my hormones started to kick in, and my brain started to decide to say well; let's start having relationships. And let's see how that side of life does. It started when I was in High School, when I like this one girl, but I never knew if she ever like me, we just stayed friends.

I notice I like women, when I was about 14 years old, it could have started when I was younger, I would always liked to dress as a guy so that women would notice me, I didn't know how to approach women. Some of the women didn't like lesbians or gays, so I had to be very careful who I ask, because I like them romatically, I could get punch out by one of the girls. I like the sensitive, loving, caring, nurture and understanding in women. I look into their eyes and saw the love and compassion, which I don't see in a man. I couldn't fall in love with a man as easily I would with a women.

In high school I was interested in girls but I was afraid to approach anyone, not knowing how they would react towards me, I wasn't a fighter I would avoid confrontations with people.

I had a boyfriend in high school, it wasn't a long term relationship, I was 16 years old he was 24 years old. My mom had found out about it, and she caught him at the gas station one day and told him to stay away from my daughter, he did, I wouldn't doubt she scared the crap out him because I never saw him again.

In high school I would help my friends when they had problems with their boyfriends, they would come to see me about what they should do, I would tell them to be honest with them and say how they feel, and it is up to that person on how they take the situation. Some of them could handle the honesty, but some couldn't handle the truth. I am a very blunt person I tell it like it is, but sometimes I knew when to hold my opinions.

About the age of sixteen I decided to run away from home, thinking no one loved me or if my parents didn't care, I felt alone. To tell you the truth, now that I think about it, I just couldn't get things done my way. Amazing when a person gets older how all the pieces fit together, people start to understand why our parents did what they do. As young people we think we know more than any one, I wished I listened more and did less on what I wanted, and more of what I needed.

I was always active with surfing, baseball, canoe paddling, and bowling; I was more of an outdoor person, I am more of that tom boyish person. I remember that when I was about nine years old, my oldest brother took me surfing, so we paddled out kind of far, well as soon as we got far enough my brother left me by myself and he went home (dirty trick) of course I started to cry. A surfer saw me and pushed me back to shore. I still went out surfing I wasn't scared, I guess my brother wanted me to not be afraid of being in the ocean.

So in love with life, God, even though I've been through a lot I always think of the blessings that is given to me, if it weren't for my pass I wouldn't of been the strong women I am today, I want to thank everyone who has taught me, and for my family being there when I needed them, I really appreciate all that they have done, to think if my family at times deny my quest for things I wouldn't of learn how to be dependent on myself.

Then at the age of 18 I was working for a towing company, I'd go to the race track and hook up the disable racing cars. When we weren't doing that we go and tow vehicles around the island, I like that job. My other brother was into racing so I help him fix engines, to get it ready for racing. I remember we were fixing this one engine on an A frame and the pulley gave out the motor fell right on my foot. Luckily my foot didn't get damage to seriously, I didn't have to get rush to the hospital. Just rub it and continued helping my brother.

Then it started my heart fell in love, for the first time in my life.

My first experience with a woman, I was excited, finally someone noticed me. She was about 32 years older then I, it was back in the middle of 1975, it was very exciting at first, but she was with someone else at the time we had met, and her girlfriend was trying to flirt with me "please I wasn't into manly women" I like famine women, at the time she was divorced, she had two homes, and three adult children. I was interested in her, being that this was my first time liking a women. I went to her house so that I could go swimming in her pool, (just an excuse to be there), she was interested in me also, because she kept watching me, where ever I go in the house or even sitting watching television. Then one day we made that big move, we finally got together as a couple, it was rough in the begining of our relationship. Because I was only 17yrs of age at the time. My parents tried to keep me from going over to her house, my parents really didn't like her, besides her girlfriend had called my parents house and told my parents if I don't stay away she will hurt me. Well at that time my girlfriend and I were heading back to her house, after having lunch and my parents were park on the side of the road waiting for us, watching for her car to drive by them, I saw my parents and we pulled over, my parent told me to get into their car so I did, not knowing of what was going on. I got home and a few minutes later I heard police cars going down the front road I lived on the back road. My parents then told me later that if I were to go to her house, her girlfriend was going to hurt me. A few days later I told my parents that I needed to get my ukulele from her house, so my dad called the police and they drove me and my dad to her house, my dad and the police officer was asking me qestions, if I was involved with her romantially, of course I told them no, we were friends, my dad couldn't look at me when he was asking me thoughs questions. When we got to the house she told my dad that he wasn't allowed on her property, my dad stood by the brick wall waiting for us. So the police officer and I went to the door to get my ukulele. I went inside and ask her, if she was ok, she said yes, I got my ukulele and left. Few days had pass and I went to her house, I left my car over my friends house so no one would see me going to her house, I caught the bus to her house. Some how my parents found out what I was doing, so I just walk to her house. I then turned 18years of age and moved in with her, one night when my parents were asleep I left.

November of 1975, in that same year we decided to move, I was excited, young and naive. I went home to my parents house, to say good-bye to my parents and to let them know I was leaving. I spoke to my father we were in the kitchen, I told him what my plans were, all he said to me, "go your nothing but trouble," I told him I love him and left. My mom didn't say much she just sat there and watch me walk out the door.

In November 1975 we flew to a different country stayed at a hotel, there was a concert across from where we were staying. The next day someting was happening out of our hotel, we had to stay in our room because there was a sniper on the roof of our hotel, we couldn't leave or room until it was clear for us to go, until the hotel manager said it was safe, finally they called our room and said it was safe, we could leave our room. We stayed in the hotel until the car that she ship over could be picked up. Once the car was ready we drove from the hotel to our destination. The roads were slippery with ice and snow, I was driving and I didn't have any experience driving on ice or snow. As we were driving I was passing this truck that was driving to slow for me, and about a mile down the road I hit black ice the car started to swerve, I tried to correct the car I couldn't, there was a mountain on one side and the embankment on the other side, the car made a 350 degree turn and we stop in the middle of the road. "At that moment I knew why the truck was going slow". The car was loaded with a lot of heavy baggage in the back and I think thats what made it stop spinning, or we just hit dry road. It took us eight hours to drive to our destination, I drove slowly.

It was beautiful with the snow and the forest trees all around. I lived in this country for seven years. I would call home every once in awhile, I even surprised my parents in coming home one Christmas. I had my older sister pick me up from the airport, so that I could surprise my mom and dad. They were happy to see me. I then went back, to where I thought was my home. I missed my family and friends at my hometown. When I called home I spoke with my brother his about two years older than me, I told him he sound different because at that time I have not heard from them about couple of years, he told me you should hear yourself, he had spoken broken English. We laugh about it and went on talking, asking how everything was doing.

I was so young and naive I didn't know any better, I worked hard and hardly went out. Then one day my girlfriend met this guy way older then her, he had money and took her places, I never thought about it cause she told me they are just friends, he use to take her to Las Vegas, we were afraid to let anyone know that her and I were lovers because of the discrimination against homosexuals.

I had a stange feeling about my girlfriend and this guy, one day I arrived home from the doctors and I had sneak around the back door, because I wanted to know if they were more then just friends. She had poodles and any sound they hear they would bark so I opened the gate very slowly, because I notice that this guys car was there parked in the drive way, so as I was walking to the back area I saw him foundling her breast. I quickly open the door and they were startled, I gave my girlfriend such a look she knew I was pissed off. I didn't say anything to neither of them and walk right to the bedroom. When he left I lost it, I started to yell at her and rip her blouse saying you want everyone to see your breast, then there you got your wish, I was so hurt, I was trusting her with this person. She started to follow me I told her to just leave me alone. I had left the house, I rented a motel room where I was working just to think things out. I cooled down because I miss her so, I went back home and things didn't seem the same. I had no trust with this women. She kept seeing this guy and plus others that I never knew until later. I finally said it was over, I called home and ask if I could come back home, this was in 1982. I woke my girlfriend up and ask her to drive me to the bus station so I can catch my airplane back home. We never talk about this situation over or to solve it, I just left. When I got home I was so sad my heart broken and yet I was still in love with her, after all she was my first women. I couldn't focus on anything I be by myself didn't want anyone near me it took me 5 years to get over it. I took care of myself I told myself I had to move on, it was such a bad experience. In 2014 I was looking on the internet, I was curious and type my ex girlfriend name and learned that she had passed away in August 2013.

Later I meet other people but wasn't involve with them just friends never serious with anyone else. Until one day I met this girl she had a baby boy, she just got out of a relationship with her boyfriend. I like her but wasn't in love with her. We lived together for maybe a month, she decided to go back with her boy friend, that was the end of that, never saw her again.

One of my friend's ex-girlfriend was interested in me and I knew it but I didn't have any feelings for her, knowing that my friend was so madly in love with her and this girl wouldn't give my friend the time of day, they gone with each other off and on for years. I knew of this kind of women cause all she was doing is using my friend and I saw right through her, this girl really like me but I knew what would happen if we were to have a relationship, she end up hurting me. So I would just go out with friends and party with them I didn't drink much maybe one or two didn't care for it, just hung out in the bars sometimes with friends or by myself, I would go out to dinner I be by myself it was ok, I join the GYM getting myself into shape I was doing good for a while to until they closed the gym, then I bought my own equipment and work out at home.

My friend and I went to this place where they took head shots, I thought it would be nice to see myself as a women.

I didn't feel comfortable made up like this I was a lot more comfortable in blue jeans and T-shirts.

Around 1989, in the bar I meet a woman, I was sitting at the bar and she sat next to me. We started to talk and she told me that I was comfortable person to talk with because I would listen to her instead of talking, I gave her my number and we parted ways. I later had a call from this women that I met at the bar, so we got together and became friends, I wanted more but she was into guys, but I was not going to give up that wasn't my nature. We finely were seeing each other but she had this one male friend that would come to her house every now and then he give her money and what she needed, but he was very careful of his money he would give her what she need, he had his own business. I was falling in love with her and wanted to be together, but that's not what she wanted. I went through a lot again but this time I got stronger. Yes, it hurts but it seems that I keep finding the wrong women for me. I fall in love to easily I need to start thinking with my head, not my heart. We had fun together; she have two girls watch I adored. Her and I would go out to gay bars and I would participate in fashion shows, I would dress in a tuxedo and then change my clothes to a swim suit, I didn't win, we had one hell of a good time.

Once again I am on my own, broken heart no where to turn, living in pain and sorrow. When will this end, I decide to go to church to find some peace with my soul. I went to counseling, read books, listen to talk shows to find myself. To change whatever I can to make my life better, to find the right person to love and to love me. I find that women are harder to please then men, it's that women seems to be more demanding than men are, I am so frustrated with these women that I don't' want to be with them anymore, it's one bad experience after another hurt after hurt. And all I wanted to be is "LOVED" is that so hard. It seems to me some of these women just don't know what they wanted at least the ones I been with, sometimes I felt like I was being used in some way or they just don't know what the heck they want, I've heard that couples stay together for 20, 40 or more years and this is men with men; women with women, what the "hell" what am I doing wrong. I may be moving too fast not getting myself knowing these people, before making a commitment.

I pray for you when I am awake
And dream of you when I am asleep
I sit in the garden as if you were beside me
When watching a movie I pretend we are cuddling
You inspire me to live on
You give me strength to wake in the morning with love in my heart
We both encourage each other to go forward in life and live it to the fullest
You are my weakness when your in my arms
And my strength when you are far
Til the day we meet with compassion and love in our eyes
May God keep you safe for me to love

Now I really made a big step I got married to man this was in somewhere in 1990's, it only lasted 1 year I wasn't in love with him and he was not in love with me, we just did it. I wasn't happy. I was just going through the motions, so was he but we had a good time the first month or so that's it, I lived mostly at home with my parents. That first year, our anniversary we had celebrated with our little wedding cake and then the divorced, WOW!!! Never did that again, not with a man. Don't get me wrong he was a good man I just wasn't into him and he wasn't into me, he wasn't gay or anything just didn't work out between us, we didn't have any love between us.

I feel my life was really mess up royal, with break ups and drama, hurt, disappointments, so I thought to myself, what is God trying to tell me or is giving me, hard core lessons on life so that I can maybe help someone in my situation, I hope so because I want it to stop. All I want is someone to love me, I know I am not an angel, I have done stupid things in my life and I pray that I didn't hurt anyone if I did I am so sorry and hope that they can find it in their hearts to forgive me, I don't do things intentionally.

My parents were loving people, everything was about family and love, and I like it when my mom use to smile and my dad he like to crack jokes made us laugh. But we had our share of butt whopping when we needed it, and we all lived through it, I have two brothers and two sisters with me a total of five siblings. We had our parent going crazy at times, they loved each one of us no matter what we did or who we became they always seen beyond what we choose in life. I thank God for giving me the parents I had in my life. When my dad got sick and was in the hospital in a coma, I visited him every day after work I sit by his bed and talk with him. I told him how much I loved him, and that we were not angry with him but the sickness he had, when he woken from the coma he seems to have more of a peaceful look on his face he seems happy. In 1999 my dad passway, then two years later my mom was in the emergency room, everyone was there but me, I had a call from my sister-in-law telling me that mom at the hospital. I rush to the hospital everyone was there, I ask my younger sister what had happen she just look at me, so I proceed to my moms room. I look at her and told her I love you its ok mom, then I saw her take her last breath, she didn't want to die until she saw everyone. They are gone now, I keep them living in my memory, my Dad left us on, August of 1999, there after my Mom on, May of 2002, I miss them so much, they were the best friends I ever had. They knew my life situation and not once they never judged us or stop loving me or my siblings. They loved us until the end and still to this day. There are time I feel my father touching my feet, because as a kid he would always tickle my feet, and I feel my mom touching the side of my face, I know its them letting me know they really haven't left, they still watching over us.

Sometimes I may not have all the answers to a problem but I try to help.

My mom said to me once, "if you can't talk to me as your mother then talk to me as your friend."

I always was open with my mother, I could tell her anything, she was a wise women…. I miss my parents, I wish I could of done more for them, I always told them I loved them.

Sometimes people take there parents for granted and never realize the meaning they have in our lives, until the day they are gone, then it's to late to appreciate the love and caring a parent has, they put all there devotion to the children, I told my parents thank you for all they have done for me, even though we had disagreements we always found a way in our heart to forgive and love each other, I am talking through experience of my own life. All I can do now is to remember what I was taught from my parents.

Sometimes in life we need to let our children grow and to be their own person, we as parent just need to stand by there decisions and pray.

Parents need to be secure with themselves in order to let their children grow, because if the parents are insecure with themselves, the children will feel the insecurity within themselves.

I wrote this after there passing......

"When my parents died, I felt Abandoned...
When I didn't hear from my sisters & brothers
I was Lost...
When my relationship was over I felt Rejected...
GOD said to me, take my hand, I will lead you
the way...to where you will not feel abandon,
lost, or rejected...But Loved, found, and cared
for...
GOD said to me, remember not all can be
perfect...that's the way of life in how we grow,
the love for how we care for each other...I can
show you the way to be stronger and wiser
in life...before GOD had departed, he said,
remember I will always be by your side to guide
you along the way...you will never be alone.
Its not about about being Abandoned, its
being Strong
Its not about Lost, its about Finding Yourself
Its not about Rejection, its about Moving
Forward."

About 1993 I meet a women in a bar she was a bar tender, of course, at a gay bar. I was interested in her, she was interested in me, her eyes would follow me when I was in the bar. One night they had country music which I like and started to learn how to do country dancing. At the bar, they had country dancing, I finally got to ask her to dance with me, my body was shaking all over as we were dancing, when we were done dancing I stood by the exit door near the bathroom when I saw her walking towards me. She ask me to come to the bar the next day and meet with her while she was working, I said ok. The next day I went to the bar where she was working, I sat at the bar having a drink when this guy came up to the bar and sat down next to me, we started talking and all of a sudden he realize that I was a female, he said to me he is so sorry I thought you were a guy, I wanted to ask you to go home with me. He was trying to pick up on me, we started to laugh about it. We sat for awhile and he went along his way. I told her what had happen she smile and went back to work it wasn't that busy.

When that bar closed down she work at a different bar, I use to wait for her when she was done working. One night this couple were arguing and we knew them, the girl sat down by me, by then her girlfriend came up and was talking to her girlfriend, they started to argue, I told the girlfriend to let it go and leave her alone. The girl grab my neck, I took her down to the floor and started hitting her, I usually sit at the bar and I would wait for my girlfriend to finish work, the owner of the bar knew me and she knows that I sit at the bar and I don't bother anyone. Well, my girlfriend came from behind the bar and was calling my name, I didn't hear anyone, it's like I black out, finally one of my friends pulled me off the girl. The girl thought I was trying to pick up on her girlfriend but she was my girlfriend cousin. The girl I was fighting with said something and my girlfriend said "Not if I have something to do with it", right then the girl knew that she was my girlfriend. My girlfriend ask me to speak with the owner of the bar and tell her what had happened, and to apologize. The next night I spoke to the owner and she told me she knows me and that I am not a trouble maker she sees me always sitting in the bar and bother no one, she accepted my apology and I was always welcome to her bar. I would help my girlfriend clean up after the bar closed.

My mom like my girlfriend because she would help my mom when she was sick. Then things started turning to the worse again, my girlfriend kept telling me she never was by herself and that what she would like to do, I push it aside and didn't think about it. We took my mom and sister to the Perry and Price show just us girls sorry dad he was not invited it was girls day out, we had a nice time. Later that year I had found out that my girlfriend not seen her daughter in 15 years so finely her daughter come to visit her mom, and I took them to the Perry and Price show, they were on the air and everything, it was nice to see them together. One Christmas eve my girlfriend and I stayed up all night putting two bikes together for her granddaughters, we were so tired we started to laugh at the silliest things, we laugh so much we had tears.

Then things began to go down hill again we were not getting alone and I told my girlfriend she had to leave, and she was happy with that, it seems that most of these women didn't have any feelings and if they did they sure hid it well, cause I never saw any of it. I wanted her back and apologize, because I was hurt of what she wanted and it wasn't me. We would have good times together but all she wanted to do was be at her friend's house every weekend and I wanted to do something different. I know she loved me, and I loved her but she wanted to move on without me we been together four years, she wanted to be single. Here I am trying to make a life commitment and it seems that the ones I am with wanted to be single....what gives!!!! It feels like I am the only one knew what the heck they want. I don't get it; many men, treated there wife's worst then I, but they stayed through it thick and thin good and bad. What is it with me?, what am I doing wrong?, I'm not a bad person, never cheated on the people I was with, didn't drink, didn't do drugs, I may get little upset and frustrated and raise my voice but nothing that would have someone not love me I give my heart whole to the person I am with, and I keep giving no matter what they done to me.

Now it's the year 2000 I meet a lady that is 20 years younger than me, she was 22 years old at the time, I felt hope! that maybe this luck of mine would change with this women, well it did a little not much. I meet her on one of these phone dating system, she called but I wasn't home, so I called her back and her mom answered the phone, she ask me who I was, I told her I was her daughter friend, her mom told me that she wasn't home. So she had called me back and we talk on the phone. We made an arrangement to meet at a mall, where I went country line dancing. We were to meet in front of McDonald's, I sat in front of McDonald's waiting for her we were to meet at 7:00 in the evening, but she was a little late which was fine, I notice this girl looking at me and I thought it was her, but it wasn't, that was a relief, it gave me more time to calm myself down. Then finely she show up she gave me a cute little wave, I loved it, her hair was curled, she wore black, she really looked good, kind of the on the shy side which was really cute I like that, she have a beautiful smile and till this day she have that smile, with her beautiful brown eyes. We went to Zippy's to have coffee, I didn't know at the time she don't care for coffee, but I know now.

She told me she have a child that is two years old, going on three.

It felt comfortable talking with her, we went on seeing each other, and in only two weeks of meeting with each other the big moment came, I ask her to be my girlfriend, she accepted. That was happiest day of my life, I was praying for a family and now I got one, I wanted a boy and now he is in my life too. When I got to meet her parents, even her sister, the sisters boyfriend and baby. Yup, they all came out to meet with me. The first one was her mom she came right into the truck gave me a kiss on the chick, and her dad holding the baby came on the driver side, I told her dad, handsome little baby just like the grandpa he started to smile. I meet everyone and then her and I left. We would cruise around with her son, in the truck.

My girlfriend and her mom once came to my job and my girlfriend made lunch for me, it was bean sprouts sandwich, and it was really good. She and I would see each other often, or talk on the phone, no matter how late it was or even if I had to work the next day I made a point to go and see her every chance I got.

Then one day her parents ask my girlfriend to move out, so I was trying to find her a place to stay even at my mom's house, but my sister the youngest one told my mom either the girl go or I go so my mom told me that my girlfriend couldn't stay there any more, I told my mom she has no one to stay with, so I got a motel for us to stay in, later her parents took her back home. Everything was going good for awhile until her parents wanted her out again. So I finely found this apartment for us to live, all three of us moved in the apartment, this was our home from now on. We still went to visit her parents we were not upset with them or anything, she loves her parents. We would go over and help them move, have BB-Q, swim in the pool at their place, go out to dinners with them, take her mom places. I would have a blast with her father, he be joking with me most of the time. He would say, "what on welfare"; he knew I have a job; they were fun to hang out with.

Her parents were trying to teach their daughter how survive, and be strong for the world out there, which she became very good in doing. She let no one push her around, when I first meet her I knew she is really intelligent person, it shows, the why she present herself. That's why I fell in Love with her; she was the loving person I was looking for all my life; she is also very beautiful person on the inside her heart, besides good looking. We had a fun and loving relationship through the many years we been together.

In 2006 I injured my back and shoulder at work, I haven't worked since, and we are now in 2011. Our relationship hasn't gotten any better neither, we would argue a lot, I would be depress because I couldn't work, we didn't do things we use to do. She kick me out so many times I went to my older sister house to where my sister told me I can't come back any more. I use to sleep in the car or just hang out at the bus stop, I had no money no clothes. I ask her if I could come back and she took me back. She and I were hoping that things would change but it just got worst. At one point she told me that she was going out to be with her class mates she said it was one female friend and a male friend. When she was getting ready to leave she told me that the girl had cancelled, and that only her and the guy were going to meet. I was so upset because she knew before going out that the girl wasn't going to be there. Well we got into an argument. I got so angry and told her, she needs to come home I am leaving, her son was sleeping I didn't want to leave him alone at home. I forgave her and went on with our life. We got into so many disagreements I can't even remember what we were fighting about anymore. The second time we were not getting along she was talking to this guy on the phone for couple of days I was still living with her and didn't even know she was trying to start another relationship with someone else, she would hide it. I took care of my girlfriend and her son as best as I could, just don't know what happened.

We go out and take her son to join basketball games, he played in the baseball little league, when he got older we got him into football, we use to go to the carnivals. I remember us taking him on a pony ride when he was small, I taught him how to swim, we enjoyed doing things with our son, we did a lot together as a family, we went hiking, bike riding, Christmas we take our son to the mall and ride the train watch him going around in circles. We didn't have all bad times we had a lot of good times too, but she said she can't remember them because the disagreements we had. I cry so much praying that things would be better with us, she tells me, that she's not in love with me anymore, and that hurts after 11 years. of struggled relationship, I may of have some part for her not loving me, I never cheated on her, would it be more within her that she took intrest with some one else, could I have done other things that I could of made it better. All I wanted is someone to love me. What hurt me the most was that she told me I am not her family.

Something I had written:

> I want someone to love me,
> Not judge me, too understand me
> Not dislike the things I do, to understand why
> I do them, Not control me of it,
> but to guide me through them,
> Not just to Love me because I am able to
> provide you with things, just love me because
> I am me

Today I am staying with her but in different rooms. I one day I had told her I can't live like this anymore that I need to leave, I didn't want to leave but it hurts to stay when someone don't love me anymore. I love her dearly, it's sad to say she doesn't love me the same anymore. On January 12, 2014 I moved out. Because she went out with her sister and cousin on Saturday, she came home about four in the morning on Sunday to bring her son home and she went back out again I ask our son who she was going out with he said her friends, I knew already it was a guy. I then ask him for my car key. I started to take all of my things and pack my car by time I was taking the last load I saw her coming home, I notice a white truck leaving. I went back up stairs and told her I saw the white truck leaving. I told her that she was seeing someone, she said that they are only friends. I told her that it could turn out to be more than friends, she said don't know that. She told me we are not attracted to each other, I didn't say anything. I didn't feel that way I am still in love with her, I told her its ok I understand, being that she was so young and had a big responsibity (her son) and no one else to help her, I feel she was missing something in her life. As I was waiting for the elevator she was calling me back to talk, I felt there was nothing else to say she already made her choice in what she wanted. I am so hurt and broken heart I fell deeply in love with her I never felt like this before with anyone, even in my other relationships. This would be the third time, I totally moved out all my things, I should known the first time not to come back. This relationship felt so different, it felt so real, because this was the first person that really loved me and her son nothing around her mattered but her family. After the break up she told me that I wasn't her family, that really hurt.

It's sad that she was deprived of her younger days, she wanted to do so much when she was in High school she wanted to play sports, and a lot of other activities, it feels as though she was deprived of these things, now that she can do them without permission, the one that loves her with all their heart and wants to spend all my life with her has to pay the price, of what her ex's did her wrong who has to suffer for it. It feels that she took it out on me, because it wasn't long when her boyfriend had done her wrong, when I meet her I felt she didn't get over what he did, and all these years I took the blame for his actions. All I could do was to love her and make her happy. Sometimes she thinks I might be like her ex's that I may not treat her or her son good, all I did was love them. I was afraid to talk to her son because she is standing right there, if she couldn't hear what I was telling him because she was in the other room, she would ask her son what I was saying to him. She didn't trust me with him, her son and I got along great, we had our little differences but we forgot about it and moved on.

I was walking on egg shells when I was with her son, but he and I would have a lot of fun. I sometimes tried to teach him street smart he didn't take some of the things to seriously and joked back with me, but he knew when I meant business, we understood each other. I do anything for the both of them. It's that sometimes I really didn't know what she wanted and it was very frustrated for me, I tried my best to do things she ask of me, I also wanted to do things I like, it was okay with me that she likes to go out with her friends I wouldn't hold her back, I wouldn't stop her in what she like to do because I'm loving her I am not her boss, to tell her it's okay to go out, she has a mind of her own. Her son and I sometimes like to do different things and not always together, we are able to do things separate, and still be a family.

I know I am not a very good house keeper, I don't clean house every day. She just gets frustrated when I don't do anything, when I do clean up the place I ask for some help to keep it clean, like wash your own dish if the sink is clean after breakfast, lunch or dinner little things so it would not be so heavy of a job for me, because I have a really bad back, I had surgery on my right shoulder because of an accident and my left shoulder I have a hard time reaching to high places now I found out that I have arthritis on my right knee and it hurts so bad I have a hard time walking but I push myself. I am the kind of person no matter how much pain I am in I try my best to do things, I may not get it done all in one day I will do as much as I can, but I guess that wasn't good enough. I am an independent person I do things for myself I rarely ask for help, when I do need help I'll ask for it.

She ask me what I want for Birthday's and Christmas, I tell her I don't know, because I have everything I need, and that's my family, I am happy with that, it's not that I need material things, I don't, I am content of what I have in my life.

I use to cook breakfast and dinner but we cook differently from each other, she would complain she don't like the way I cook, I sometimes didn't like what she cooks but I would eat it, then her son started to complain as well about how I cook so I stop cooking, she cooks for herself and her son, I cook for myself, I had no problem with cooking for myself. There were times I know she was tired because she comes home from work and she is tired so I treat both of them to dinner. I would get up in the mornings I got her lunch and breakfast ready for work, then I would make her sons breakfast before he went to school. I drove her son to school every day and I pick him up after school, there were times he walk with his friends home from school, I would pick up my girlfriend from work every day, unless she went out with her friends then she would take her car to work and I would use my car to drive her son to and from school.

> Promise to be, thinking of you
> making our life better together,
> praying to GOD to give us the strength and wisdom, to make our love strong in our life together, to never give up on each other
> ...to be with you planning, sharing our future and dreams
> with you, raising our children to be better people in life,
> doing my part in life to make you happy, I want to assure you that I will be enjoying every moment with you in life, not to miss a heartbeat
> "ALWAYS LOVING YOU"

I wrote this the first time we broke up, I was so lost without her, I couldn't sleep or eat I lost a lot of weight, at that time I didn't have a vehicle I rode my bike or I caught the bus, my head wasn't screwed on right. Every time she would call me to help her I would go right away no matter what time of day or night it was. There was one night she called and told me that her car wouldn't start, I got my tools and walk to the bus stop and went to her house. When I got to her house the vehicle needed a battery so all three of us caught the bus to the store and rode the bus back with the battery, got her car fix. There were times she was having problems with her son and she would call me, I would go over to talk with him, we got everything straighten out together. Even if I weren't living with her we would solve problems together.

In 2012 we went to Las Vegas, I wasn't feeling well, for some reason I got sick. When we got to Las Vegas she would be off by themselves, she told me before we left that don't except us to hang around you, I said fine, you guys do your thing and I'll do mine, we went to shows and wax museums walk around together.

At one point she got so upset with me because it was a little hot and we walked, she really got upset. We walk the strip and she wouldn't want to walk with me, I was so hurt during this trip but I tried to make the best of it. I tried so hard to make her happy but no matter what I did it was wrong.

> Keep me from pain,
> Shelter me from harm
> And fill me with all your charm

At times I would cry when I was by myself because I knew she was slowly stopped loving me. The more I tried the worst it got.

I would say good morning and good-bye when she left for work, she would say the same but she wouldn't look at me. She was acting like she hates me. They were lots of good times that we shared; we would sit in the bedroom and talk about the pass, when her parents were alive.

We had our share of up and downs, we cried and laugh, most of all we had each other.
Being without you
Is like heaven without
ANGELS!

In 2011 I got certified as a dog trainer, it took me one year to do the course. I did half of the school work when I was living at home the other half when I moved out, and finish at my brothers house. Between all the dramas I was going through, I was going to finish something in my life. Working with animals is my passion, I always dream of owning a farm with lots of different animals.

It was hard but I made it. Big thanks to my sister-in-law if it wasn't for her I didn't know what to do. All the crying and anger she sat through it all for two years. I also have a very good friend that took the drama I was going through, if it weren't for the both of them I be so lost. Thank GOD for loving family and good friends, are hard to come by.

I wish I had someone say to me, that life does have its ups and downs and that you need to pick your relationships carefully, get to know them first. It does not matter most of the relationships I had I got to know them before commitment and it still didn't work out with us. It depends on the individual, if they are not happy with themselves it not going to work out.

Living with my ex-girlfriend I was pick on for everything I did, it seems I did nothing right. I would clean house but I couldn't move anything around that didn't belong to me. Or put it in a different place or if I didn't put things back the way it was, so I give up I was tired of being yell at for something that was senseless. I would cook and that wasn't even right, no matter if I cooked the way they like, what is a person to do. What kept me going are the good times we had doing things with our son, and things I did with her.

I was becoming very unhappy, but I loved her with all my heart, I kept trying but whatever I did to make her happy wasn't working.

I talk with her every now and then, but she needs to figure out what she wants I gave her the space she wants. She tells me that she wants to get to know people before making a commitment. We had the chance to get to know each other for 11 years, we accepted each other. I feel it does not matter how long you take to get to know someone we never get to really know them. I thought we be together until death do we part.

We never know what the future holds, all I wanted is someone to love me, and I to love them.

I read books, seen counselors, listen to Dr. Laura, now my strength is God. I ask for strength, wisdom and forgiveness. It's going to take some time to get over her, and I know one day I will find the strength to let go, and move on, my heart fell so deeply in love with her it's hard for me to move on right now, but I will. I don't want to set myself up for another disappointment and hurt again, there is someone out in the world that has love for me, that special someone will walk into my life and love me for who I am. It wouldn't be fair to the person, if I were to start a relationship at this moment. I gone through enough pain and sorrow it's time someone to love me as I would love them, who is willing to share the rest of our lives together, and cherish every moment we breath in life.

HONEY, I LOVE YOU SO MUCH!!!!
I'd DIE for you....I'd TAKE A BULLET for you
I'd GO TO JAIL for you
"BUT I AM DAM IF I' LL TAKE YOUR CRAP!!!"
Written by Janice Pruse

August 2014 I moved out of my brother's house, I found me a cute little duplex one bedroom house. I love it I can have my doggies, which I wanted for a long time.

My ex girlfriend and I are seeing each other but we are not in relationship, we get along better now, since we are not living together. She still goes on dates, I can't say anything about it we are not committed to each other. I told her that I would start to date, she was not happy about it, I told her, wow you can date but it's not okay with me to date. She later told me that I supported her and that she should do the same, I can tell that she is not agreeable with this arrangement. I am not ready to be with anyone at this moment I just want to go out and meet different people and enjoy myself. I have not dated any one for 4 years, with our on and off again relationship, even when we were not together I haven't dated anyone till this day.

It's been a long hard road for me, I just wanted to just run and hide. There been days to where I just wanted to sit and cry, but I couldn't tears wouldn't come out, I just got stronger every time I would be thinking about the situation I kept going. I had so much on my plate it was spilling over, and there were times I felt that I was losing my sense of direction. I knew I have a purpose on this earth and I was not giving up, I fought and I fought hard, even with all the disappointments I gave it my all, I did have a lot of support from my older sister, and my brother the one I was living with, God Bless my whole family and friends even the ones that didn't support me, their my family and I love them all, no matter what some of them may have done or said about me, they are family.

Despite with all that had happen in my life I still have a good loving heart, I still care for everyone, it's my calling to be good to everyone no matter what they may have done to me I forgive them with all my heart, most important I forgive myself. That is the how I move on with life is to forgive, as Jesus forgave us.

Around October 2015 we got my girlfriend and her son puppies, I bought 2 males half pit bull and something else we don't know what breed it is, but they are so cute, and playfull. Later we were given a pure bred female blue nose pit bull by my ex girlfriend sister. My ex named her puppy Anela, I had the hardest time remembering her name my ex would always laugh at me because I would miss pronounce her name, after a month or so I finally got it right. In March Anela got very sick we took her to the veterinarian and found out from altera sound that she had a deformity kidney, she would have died sooner or later, I called my ex and told her we're at the veterinarian's to put Anela to sleep, that she needs to come to the veterinarian's office, I didn't want to put Anlea to sleep until my ex arrived at the hopital. Anela was my ex girlfriend puppy, I took care of Anela because where my ex live they don't allow pets. When we first got Anela she was only two pounds two ounces, she ended up being 30 pounds when she passaway. This was a very sad day. We stayed in the room until she was gone, she laid there like she was sleeping, her back was toward us, as if she didn't want us to see her go, she went so peacefully, she didn't make a sound, then she was gone, so quickly. My ex was always afraid of dogs, Anela changed her heart about dogs, my ex is not afraid of dogs now because of the love she had for anela.

After the passing of Anela, my ex and I parted. We talk and she use to come over, but we started not to get along once again. She told me she didn't want the same sex relationship any more, we were together for 11 years, lived apart for four years. she had been dating other men, but would sleep with me. Then one day she told me she don't want to be in a relationship any more, she had found someone else, she knew him from high school. I was so heart broken, she just had finished washing her clothes at my house and was going to the laundratte to dry her clothes, she ask if I was coming with her, at this moment I was so hurt I told her to go, she said why, I told her to go and go home after she was done. I love her so much and it hurts to have my heart broken over and over by her.

March of 2015, she is now with a man that she known at high school. We had lunch twice since then, the first lunch went well. We talked and she said that if it don't work out with this guy that she got my number. I ask her not to call or text me since she was involve with this guy. The next day she text me asking me for money, which I didn't have to give her. At lunch I told her to ask her boyfriend, to borrow money. we had lunch the second time, I ask if this guy knew about us having lunch she told me no he does not know, but he knows we talk, she said its not like were doing anything. I told her she not being honest with him, and said I wouldn't like it if this was done to me. She got upset and said we came to talk about my sons graduation, which that is why we were having lunch. She told me, were not here to talk about us were here to talk about the graduation, she wouldn't let me express how I felt, I stood up and said lunch is over we never even got to eat. I left and she was still sitting there, I later called her on the phone and left a message, I said I was sorry what had happen at the dinner, because she told me not to call her or her son. I called later and said she has no control over me or her son, if he wants to talk to me it would be up to him he is 18 years of age, I told her she just lost her best friend, she called me but I was to upset and hurt to talk to her, we never spoke since then. Later she would text me on how I was doing. I went to our sons graduation, her boyfriend was there, it didn't bother me at all to see her boyfriend there at the graduation. I was there for my son no one else.

I have a new love in my life now.
I wrote these poems for her;

All I need is someone to love.....
for them to love me. I may not be the prefect person I am only human and will make mistakes. All I can do is love

the person I am with....do my best in making that person happy....also myself. I can not be you and you can not be me......we only can be ourselves. I need someone who will commit themselves to me .....as I will commit to them. I love having a family....that is very important to me. Sometimes it may not be shown but the love is there.

> You are my strength, my light, my inspiration
> When I think of you nothing else matters
> Your in my heart, my soul
> You gave me a wonderful gift and it's you
> You are my gift of life and love

May we find someone who loves us, and never part from each other, whether it's good or bad, we will learn about one another.

I went on a dating site and found me a beautiful Ukrainian women, we been writing each other for two years now, I had video chats with her, I saw who she really looks like, and I'm impressed of how she looks!

She wants to come to America to visit, but it takes very long time to get approved.

Chaos happened, the war!!! Now there is a war in Ukraine with Russia, now it's going to be very difficult for her to travel to me, the first attempt to leave her country was unsuccessful, she had to turn around and go back home, the second attempt was a little more successful, she went further then the first attempt, but the Ukrainian military stop people from going through, for some unknown reason. I'm waiting for a letter from her hopefully that she makes it to Poland.

I wrote her this prayer:

> Heavenly Father please watch over (her name),
> to guide her into a safe path, please send your
> angels to walk beside her every step of the way
> on earth,
> Heavenly Father, I am asking you for your
> forgiveness of my sins.....
> I thank you and appreciate everyday for my
> life and what you have given me......
> Heavenly Father for you are my savior......
> Amen

Most every time when I write her I send her a prayer written by me.

It's been three months now, and my girlfriend said that she is 10% of the way to Poland, she is getting closer.

Now she is having a hard time finding gasoline for the vehicle. I wrote her a letter, because it's been a while since she had wrote me to update what was going on with her.

"It's been a long struggle for me, and I know it's hasn't been easy for you, I am so afraid that I will not find love in the age that I am now, each passing day it gets scary, will I ever hold the one I love or is time just going to pass me by? Am I going to make passionate love to the women I dream of nightly?

Is this a dream or is it reality, if this is a dream please awaken me and tell me it's real, of what we have between us, or do I just keep dreaming?

My life has been nothing but dreams and hope, dream that some day someone will awaken me and love me, hopefully my dreams and hopes come true, for my heart is sad now, praying soon it will be filled with love and joy."

She confessed to me that she had the chance to arrive to America before the war, but she decided to wait, so that she could sell her house.

Sometimes it feels like a whole lot of promises, dreams.

As of today I am looking for love and the right women to love

When someone prays to God for many years, to have that special someone to be in your life, and your prayer has been answered, don't take it for granted because God had put both of you together for the reason that it was meant to be, it didn't just happen. God knows what his plans are for the both of you, it up to the both of you to figure it out, live life the best way you can. To share the good time, to help each other thru the hard times, love one another. To look into each other eyes as though its was the first time you saw each other, this should be every day of your lives together. Remember only God Knows what is ahead of you, make the best of life as you can, because God will never leave our side. Don't run thru life, walk so every moment would be remembered. Because by the time we are old, people won't say where did the time go, it only seems like yesterday we were young, or look at our children, and say I can't believe they were just babies, now they have grown so fast!!! take time to enjoy everything in life.

July 3, 2014 Written by Janice Pruse

Yes, our children they will always be our little ones no matter how old they are......my mom called me her baby even though I was in my fourties' I was still her little girl. Parents never want there children to grow, because one day knowing they will leave, but children never leave they just start a new life, and parents are still included in there life, but not as much. You have done your part in there young life, now it's our turn to live, it's not being selfish it's starting to live again, and still be involved with our children, it seems that parents been doing this generation after generation, some parents needs to give children some room so that they can spread there wings!

If they are in love than let them be, you love your children then let them be happy, no one can change their mind, their mind is already set in what they want.

Sometimes I may not have all the answers to a problem but I try to help.

My mom said to me once, "if you can't talk to me as your mother then talk to me as your friend."

I always was open with my mother, I could tell her anything, she was a wise women.... I miss my parents, I wish I could of done more for them, I always told them I loved them.

Sometimes people take there parents for granted and never realize the meaning they have in our lives, until the day they are gone, then it's to late to appreciate the love and caring a parent has, they put all there devotion into the children, I told my parents thank you for all they have done for me, even though we had disagreements we always found a way in our heart to forgive and love each other, I am talking through experience of my own life. All I can do now is to remember what I was taught from my parents.

Sometimes in life we need to let our children grow and to be their own person, we as parent just need to stand by there decisions and pray.

Parents need to be secure with themselves in order to let their children grow, because if the parents are insecure with themselves the children will feel the insecurity within themselves. Sometimes in life we need to let our children grow and to be their own person, we as parents just need to stand by there decisions and pray.

The question is what do you want in life now?

It's time to explore and fall in love with the right person.

I know for some people it may be a little difficult being with the same sex, because some never thought about being with the same sex, it may feel strange at first, hopefully they will get use to it, if you decide that this is what you want in life!

I had no problem being with with a woman it came natural, It be your choice

All I know it's a different feeling, loving a women then a man.

Women are more sensitive to their feelings and can comfort each other.

Shouldn't rush into a relationship that you don't feel comfortable with.

I know that a lot of people don't like homosexual, but now a days people are accepting that kind of life style, because there are a lot of people that are homosexual. And I am sure in other countries there are some but haven't come out and express themselves because it's not lawful in a certain country. In my country it's very open, they hold hands go out and do things like any couples would do.

I know that some people may not understand, but it's not what other's want in other peoples lives it be the person themselves who decide what makes them happy.

Some how people connect for a reason, we don't know what the outcome is going to be, but at least people tried, weather they are heterosexual or homosexual there might be a lesson in this, we will never know unless it's given a chance, sometimes the unknown is scary, but the effort can be rewarding.

If you can see yourself happy, it's something to think about.

I'm hopeful that I may have found someone in Ukraine, and that this is real.

Now it's the beginning of the winter, and a lot of people are going without warm clothes and heating systems. There's a lot of people who's been volunteering there lives to help.

Good deeds comes from the heart, not because they want too.......not because it makes them feel good about themselves, it's because of caring and love within the heart. It's giving part of yourself for the needs of others who may not be able to help themselves.

If I were to be in Ukraine I would be helping because I care for people no matter who they are. This is why I donate food to the church, because they help the people in need.

I look at my life and I am thankful for what I have, because someone else may not be so blessed, I don't complain, but I ask for everyone else to be blessed as I am. I'm not rich, I'm not poor, but I have enough to live comfortably.

I was homeless once and had no one to help me, ever since my parents died, but everyday I thanked God for the things I had and not complain about the things that I didn't have, now I have a home, God was giving me a Path that he created, I just needed to have patience.

Good will come to those who will understand the path of life.

I may not know the hardship of the war and what people are going through, I understand the pain and suffering.

And it's people who volunteer their life to the people who need it makes the world a better place to live.

My heart goes out to Ukraine and all the people from this war, Russia people is also suffering with this war.

I know with the winter coming it's going to be difficult for the children, old and the sick, because of not enough heating and warm clothes, medicine, water and food.

Hopefully that all of this chaos ends so that my lady and I may go forward in life. It seems that this is another obstacles that I will have to achieve in life.

Sometimes I unintentionally do things that may hurt someone feelings, not knowing what I had done, I want to be considerate of their emotions and feelings, as they would do the same for me.

> When the birds sing, I hear your voice
> When the sun is shining, I see your smile
> When it's dark and cloudy, I feel your pain
> When it's raining, I see your tears
> When your silence, I feel your fear

I am a person who forgives easily, I don't hold any grudges or anger inside. I like the ocean it calms me when watching the waves, most of my life I use to go to the ocean and meditate, I use to think of my life of what had happened and how to make it better. I've lost so much in my life, my parents, family, friends, and my love life. But none of these stop me from loving anyone, I am a person that never gives up on myself or other's, but it seems my pass relationships has given up on me, because they didn't want me in their lives, they felt that they could of found someone better than I. Now it's time to start my life fresh with someone who will truly love me as I am, loving, caring, honest, who has never cheated on my spouse. I'm not saying I am perfect, but good enough to love someone the way it should be.

Share each other feelings, don't hold it in your heart, communicate with one another!

Be confident, my heart, because the Lord has been good to me. - Psalm 116:7

All poems were written by me, everything is a true story.

Printed in the United States
by Baker & Taylor Publisher Services